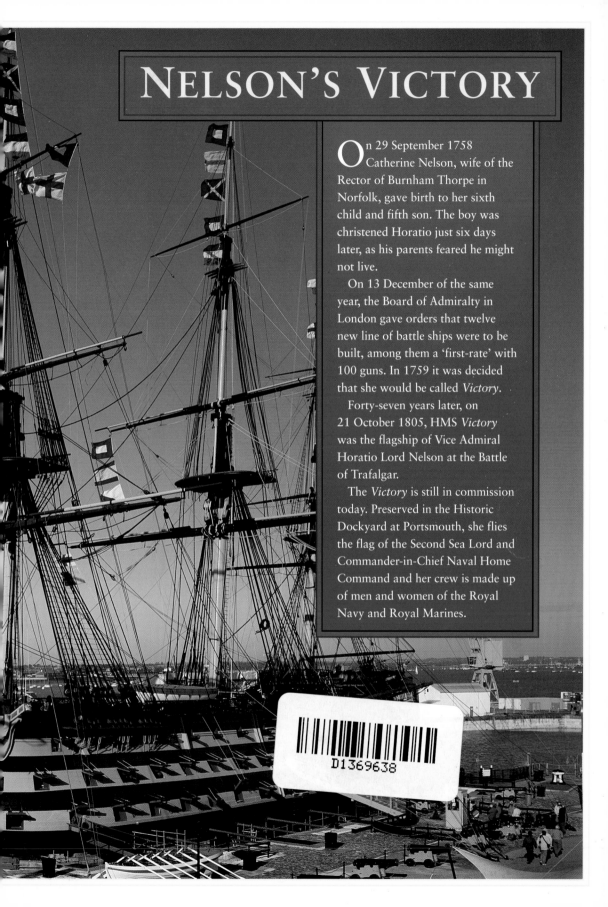

NELSON'S VICTORY

On 29 September 1758 Catherine Nelson, wife of the Rector of Burnham Thorpe in Norfolk, gave birth to her sixth child and fifth son. The boy was christened Horatio just six days later, as his parents feared he might not live.

On 13 December of the same year, the Board of Admiralty in London gave orders that twelve new line of battle ships were to be built, among them a 'first-rate' with 100 guns. In 1759 it was decided that she would be called *Victory*.

Forty-seven years later, on 21 October 1805, HMS *Victory* was the flagship of Vice Admiral Horatio Lord Nelson at the Battle of Trafalgar.

The *Victory* is still in commission today. Preserved in the Historic Dockyard at Portsmouth, she flies the flag of the Second Sea Lord and Commander-in-Chief Naval Home Command and her crew is made up of men and women of the Royal Navy and Royal Marines.

D1369638

Nelson's day cabin: in the centre is the table at which he wrote his famous last prayer.

THE SHIP

First-rate Battleships

Fighting ships of the sailing era navy were divided into six 'rates', according to the number of guns they carried and the size of their crews.

The first-rates were the largest and most powerful type of warship afloat. They carried over a hundred guns and more than eight hundred officers and men.

Their main function was to deliver shattering 'broadsides' from their powerful batteries of guns arranged in tiers on three decks. They were also often used as headquarters for an Admiral and his staff because of the extra space available. When an Admiral was on board, his presence was indicated by flying a special flag and so an Admiral's ship became known as the 'flagship'.

Nelson in his Cabin by Charles Lucy: although painted posthumously in 1853, all Nelson's surviving officers signed a testimonial to say that this portrait was a very accurate likeness of their great commander.

Building the Victory

The *Victory* was designed by the Senior Surveyor of the Navy, Thomas Slade. Her keel was laid in No. 2 Dock at Chatham Dockyard on 23 July 1759 under the supervision of the Master Shipwright, Edward Allen.

Over two thousand oak trees were used in the construction of her hull – equivalent to about 60 acres of forest. Her final cost was £63,176 (about £50 million).

The proposal to name her *Victory* was not universally popular. The previous ship of that name had sunk with all hands off the Scillies in 1744 and so sailors believed the name was unlucky. But the new ship was begun at the height of the Seven Years War, when Britain was struggling against the combined might of France and Spain. The year 1759 saw a remarkable series of British victories on land and at sea. So, in the end, she was named *Victory* after all and was given a splendid figurehead commemorating the '*annus mirabilis*' ('wonderful year').

The victories of 1759 reduced the need for new ships, so the building of the *Victory* proceeded very slowly and she was not launched until Tuesday 7 May 1765. The long period of weathering meant that her hull timbers were very well seasoned and this was one of the main reasons why she survived for so long.

By the time of her launch the Seven Years War was over and so she was placed 'in ordinary' (in reserve). It was not until 1778, when the War of American Independence broke out, that she was finally completed and prepared for active service. Fitted with a full set of masts, 27 miles of rigging and some 4 acres of canvas sails, she was also, for the first time, equipped with guns – 104 in all.

Active Service

The *Victory* was one of the most successful first-rates ever built. The excellent design of her underwater lines made her nimble and manageable despite her size and, in the right conditions, she could sail as fast as many of her smaller consorts. These qualities made her a popular ship and she was always in demand.

In 1803 she underwent a major refit that gave her a new lease of life and completely changed her outward appearance. As a result, she remained in active service almost constantly between 1778 and 1812 – a unique record for a ship of her type.

Her popularity meant that Admirals often asked to have her as their flagship, the most famous being Augustus Keppel, Richard Kempenfelt, Richard Howe, Samuel Hood and John Jervis. She also took part in many different operations, including the battle of Ushant (1781), the relief of Gibraltar (1782), the Battle of St Vincent (1797) and the two Baltic campaigns of 1808–10 and 1811–12.

However, the peak of her career came when she was Nelson's flagship in the Mediterranean from September 1803 until the battle of Trafalgar on 21 October 1805.

Keppel

Kempenfelt

Jervis

Howe

With a fresh wind astern and her sails filling, the *Victory* speeds across the Bay of Biscay en route for the Mediterranean in 1803 to become Nelson's flagship (painting by John Chancellor).

Sailing the Victory

The *Victory* carried thirty-two different sails. These were mostly hung from horizontal 'yards' mounted on her four masts (from bow to stern: the bowsprit, the foremast, the mainmast and the mizenmast). Various combinations of these sails were used, according to the strength and direction of the wind.

In order to catch as much of the wind as possible the yards were moved by a complex system of special ropes. The sails themselves were set and adjusted by members of the crew who climbed aloft, using rope-ladders fixed to the heavy ropes (or shrouds) supporting the masts, and stood on flimsy footropes, slung underneath each yard. They needed to have the agility and sense of balance of a modern-day trapeze artist.

There were no powered machines on board. All the heavy work – such as raising the yards or hoisting the huge and heavy anchors – had to be done by the men, hauling on the ship's two capstans. Not surprisingly, one of the main injuries suffered by the sailors was rupture.

The Battle of St Vincent, 14 February 1797: HMS *Victory* (centre), flying the flag of Admiral Sir John Jervis at her mainmast, fires a broadside into the stern of the Spanish *Principe de Asturias*.

The Victory *in Battle*

When the enemy was sighted, the Royal Marine drummer would sound a special drum roll: 'Beat to Quarters!' – the modern 'Action Stations!'. At once the crew would begin to clear for action – dismantling all the officers' cabins and stowing away furniture and personal belongings, so as to leave the guns completely free of any obstructions. A well-trained crew could clear a ship the size of the *Victory* in about ten minutes.

The guns would then be manned. Each one had its own crew – typically twelve men and a boy, known as the 'powder monkey', who collected the gunpowder-filled cartridges from the magazines deep in the bowels of the ship, below the waterline.

The guncrew would go through a complicated drill to prepare their guns for firing. The Royal Navy practised this drill constantly and, by the time of Trafalgar, most British warships could fire a broadside every ninety seconds – about twice as fast as their opponents. These fast and deadly hailstorms of fire gave the British an important advantage in any battle.

Boarders away! This view of the crew of HMS *Surprise* recapturing HMS *Hermione* from the Spaniards in 1799 captures the ferocity of hand-to-hand fighting.

A 'broadside' was a discharge of all the guns from one side of a ship. The guns were very rarely fired all at once, as the shock was too great a strain on the ship's timbers. More usually the guns were fired one by one from bow to stern in a ripple effect.

Three main types of shot were used in the guns: 'round shot', to batter the hull of an enemy ship; 'dismantling shot', to tear down the rigging of an opponent; and 'anti-personnel shot', to kill or maim members of the opposing crew.

Wooden ships were very buoyant, so they rarely sank in battle. Instead, they had to be captured by boarding parties. Most naval battles began as gunnery duels and ended with close-quarter hand-to-hand fighting between the crews of individual ships wedged alongside each other. In these often murderous contests cutlasses, pistols and boarding pikes were used, with covering musket fire from the Royal Marines.

THE MEN

The Ship Hierarchy

Over 850 officers and men served in HMS *Victory* at the Battle of Trafalgar. Each had a clearly defined set of duties to perform.

Since the *Victory* was usually a flagship, the chief officer was the Admiral. His task was to organize the daily affairs of the fleet and to prepare his subordinates for battle. He played very little part in the running of the ship itself. This was the responsibility of the Captain, who was assisted by his Lieutenants, each of whom looked after a particular aspect of the ship's routine – such as signalling or gunnery. The junior, or trainee, officers (known as Midshipmen) also helped with these duties. Additionally, there were a number of specialist officers, such as the Purser, who looked after the supplies, and the Master, who was responsible for navigating the ship.

The main body of the ship's company was made up of the seamen. They were divided into Able and Ordinary Seamen (the most experienced) and Landsmen (men who had little previous experience at sea). There were also boys on board, some of them as young as ten or twelve years of age; they were usually orphans who had been set to sea to learn a trade.

Finally, there was a detachment of some 150 Royal Marines. This élite corps of men was used to maintain discipline on board, and in battle they provided accurate small arms fire.

THE ADMIRAL
Vice Admiral Horatio, Lord Nelson, KB

Going to sea at the age of twelve, Nelson rose rapidly and was a full Captain at only twenty-one. He demonstrated his ability early and was rewarded with independent commands when he was still in his thirties. His unique run of decisive victories at the Nile (1798), Copenhagen (1801) and Trafalgar (1805) came at a time when the war against France was going badly elsewhere for Britain and her allies and made him an international hero. His wounds and slight stature gave him an air of frailty; but he was a man of great vitality and enthusiasm, with a special gift for inspiring others which made him one of the most successful military leaders in history. Although a skilled tactician and strategist, it was his human qualities which made him so popular in his lifetime and which have ensured him a place in British hearts that he retains to this day. As one of his officers put it: 'Nelson was the man to love'.

THE CAPTAIN
Captain Thomas Hardy

Hardy served with Nelson in all his great battles and was Captain of HMS *Victory* from 1803 until she returned to England after Trafalgar. Born in 1769, he entered the Navy in 1790, became a Lieutenant in 1793 and first served with Nelson in the frigate *Minerve* in 1796. From then on their careers were closely intertwined and Nelson came to rely very much on Hardy, both professionally and personally. It was Hardy who witnessed Nelson's last will and who later, in a famous and moving scene, kissed him farewell as he lay dying. He was made a Baronet as a reward for his part in the Battle of Trafalgar, became an Admiral in 1825, and finished his active career as First Sea Lord, before finally becoming Governor of Greenwich Hospital. He died in 1839.

THE LIEUTENANT
Lieutenant George Bligh

The son of a naval officer, George Bligh joined the Navy aged just ten in 1794 and went to sea in a ship commanded by his father. He was promoted to Lieutenant in 1801 and joined the *Victory* when she was commissioned at Chatham in 1803, after her major refit. At Trafalgar, he was in command of a division of the *Victory*'s guns and was badly wounded in the head by a musket ball. He was promoted to the rank of Commander as a reward for his services. Recovering from his wound, he continued to serve throughout the remainder of the war. He died on Trafalgar Day 1834 and was buried in the family vault in the church at Alverstoke, Gosport, within a cannon shot of where the *Victory* lies today.

THE SPECIALIST OFFICER
Master Thomas Atkinson
Born in 1767, Atkinson became a Master in the Royal Navy in 1795. In 1801 he was Master of HMS *Elephant* when she was Nelson's temporary flagship at the Battle of Copenhagen. Nelson was impressed by his navigational skills displayed during the battle and from then on the two men always served together. He became Master of the *Victory* in 1803 and served in her at the Battle of Trafalgar. After taking part in Nelson's funeral, Atkinson returned to sea until 1810, when he was appointed Second Master-Attendant of Portsmouth Dockyard. He became First Master in 1823 and remained in office until his death in 1836.

THE SEAMAN
Ordinary Seaman George Aunger
Born in Exeter in 1782, George Aunger volunteered for service in the Navy at Woolwich in May 1803 and served in the *Victory* throughout the Trafalgar campaign. After the *Victory*'s return to England, he was transferred, like many of his colleagues, to HMS *Ocean*, and served under Nelson's friend and second-in-command, Vice Admiral Cuthbert Collingwood. Eventually Aunger became a pensioner at the Royal Naval Hospital at Greenwich and remained there until his death.

THE ROYAL MARINE
Sergeant James Secker
Like Nelson, Secker was a Norfolk man, born in Norwich in 1781. He joined the *Victory* as a Sergeant in her contingent of Royal Marines in April 1803 and served in her throughout the Trafalgar campaign. He was on the quarterdeck when Nelson was shot and helped to carry him below to the cockpit. He took part in Nelson's great funeral procession through London on 9 January 1806 and then returned to barracks at Chatham.

The Death of Nelson by Benjamin West: West painted this vivid and complex picture as a tribute to Nelson and the men who fought with him at Trafalgar. Although not an accurate depiction of the scene (Nelson died, not on the quarterdeck, but in the cockpit, four decks below) it is none the less a valuable historical document since almost every figure in it is a portrait. It therefore gives us an idea of what the *Victory*'s ship's company looked like at the Battle of Trafalgar.

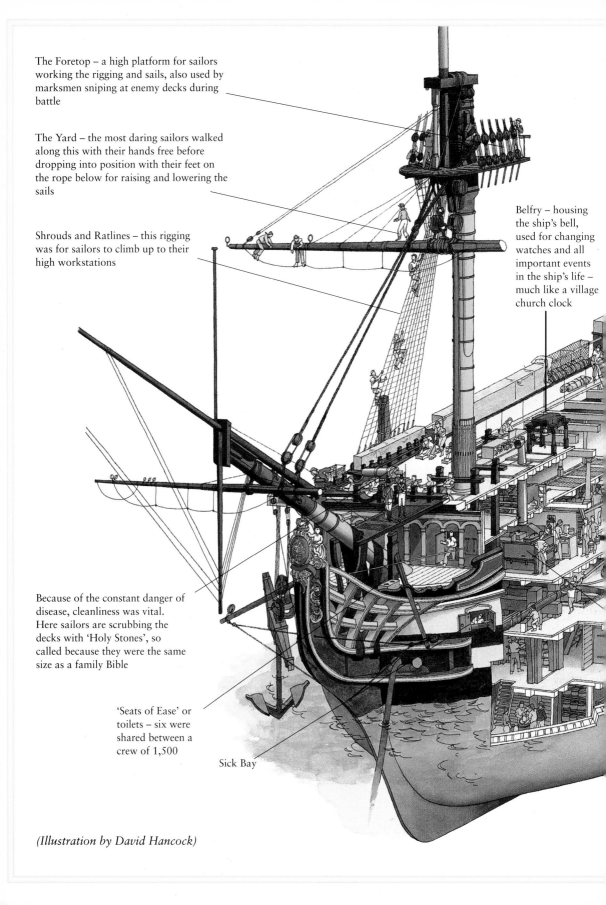

The Foretop – a high platform for sailors working the rigging and sails, also used by marksmen sniping at enemy decks during battle

The Yard – the most daring sailors walked along this with their hands free before dropping into position with their feet on the rope below for raising and lowering the sails

Shrouds and Ratlines – this rigging was for sailors to climb up to their high workstations

Belfry – housing the ship's bell, used for changing watches and all important events in the ship's life – much like a village church clock

Because of the constant danger of disease, cleanliness was vital. Here sailors are scrubbing the decks with 'Holy Stones', so called because they were the same size as a family Bible

'Seats of Ease' or toilets – six were shared between a crew of 1,500

Sick Bay

(Illustration by David Hancock)

HMS VICTORY

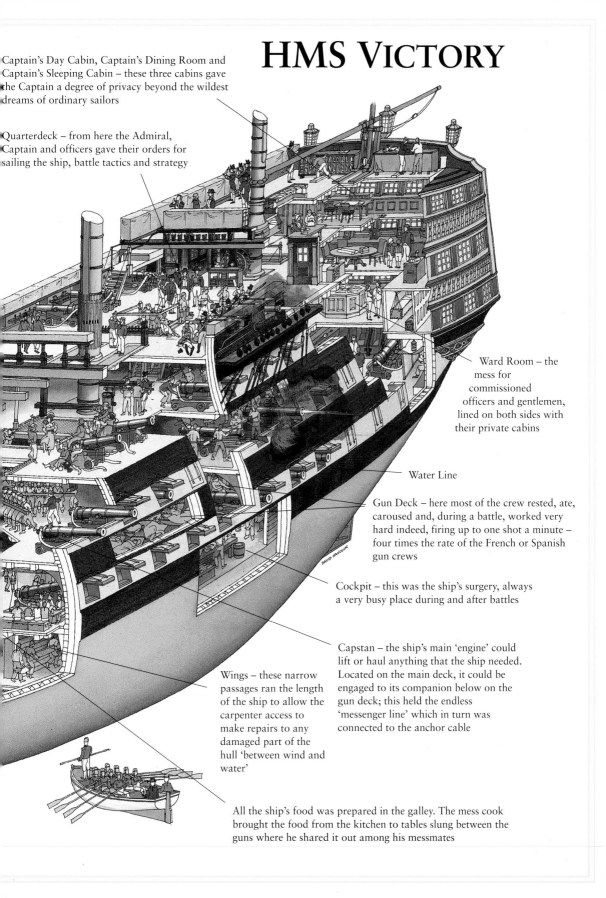

Captain's Day Cabin, Captain's Dining Room and Captain's Sleeping Cabin – these three cabins gave the Captain a degree of privacy beyond the wildest dreams of ordinary sailors

Quarterdeck – from here the Admiral, Captain and officers gave their orders for sailing the ship, battle tactics and strategy

Ward Room – the mess for commissioned officers and gentlemen, lined on both sides with their private cabins

Water Line

Gun Deck – here most of the crew rested, ate, caroused and, during a battle, worked very hard indeed, firing up to one shot a minute – four times the rate of the French or Spanish gun crews

Cockpit – this was the ship's surgery, always a very busy place during and after battles

Capstan – the ship's main 'engine' could lift or haul anything that the ship needed. Located on the main deck, it could be engaged to its companion below on the gun deck; this held the endless 'messenger line' which in turn was connected to the anchor cable

Wings – these narrow passages ran the length of the ship to allow the carpenter access to make repairs to any damaged part of the hull 'between wind and water'

All the ship's food was prepared in the galley. The mess cook brought the food from the kitchen to tables slung between the guns where he shared it out among his messmates

Recruitment

Over half the ship's company at Trafalgar were volunteers. While all the officers were full-time professionals, all the boys and Royal Marines had joined voluntarily. Moreover, some two hundred of the sailors had joined up of their own accord.

However, as in all wars, there were never enough volunteers to man all the ships required and so conscription was necessary. In the eighteenth century there were two main methods: the 'quota', by which each county in Britain was required to supply a set number of men for the Navy, and 'impressment', whereby parliament would pass special laws allowing the Navy to compel certain clearly defined types of men with maritime experience to serve in warships. This process was usually enforced by the infamous 'press-gangs' – armed bodies of sailors and Royal Marines who roamed the streets of seaports looking for likely recruits.

The Admiral's suite, with the dining cabin in the foreground, where Nelson held his famous pre-battle dinner parties. Beyond is his day cabin, where he worked through his piles of official papers.

A single hammock swings over a messtable in the cramped quarters of the *Victory*'s lower gundeck. In 1805 this tiny space would have been 'home' to at least twelve men who ate at the table and slept in shoulder-to-shoulder hammocks slung overhead.

Some unwilling sailors are captured by a press-gang operating at Tower Hill, London.

Living Conditions

Life at sea has always been hard. The *Victory*'s men lived in conditions that seem appalling to people used to central heating and refrigerated food. But, judged against living standards ashore at the time, they were not particularly uncomfortable. The main difference, of course, was the cold and damp: rheumatism was a very common complaint.

There was also very little personal privacy. Only the most senior officers had their own suite of rooms. The Admiral occupied a beautiful set on the upper gun-deck, consisting of a day cabin, dining cabin and smaller sleeping cabin, with additional space for his servants. Above these was a similar but smaller set for the Captain, with doors opening straight on to the quarterdeck, so that he could quickly reach his command position in case of an emergency. The Lieutenants and Specialist Officers had tiny sleeping cabins; but for recreation and eating they shared the large wardroom below the Admiral's suite on the middle gun-deck. All these officers had access to relatively private toilets in the 'quarter galleries' that hung out over the side at the ship's stern.

Everyone else in the ship lived, ate and slept communally – most of them on the lower gun-deck, where they slept in hammocks slung from the beams and ate at messtables erected between the guns. At sea the gunports were usually closed, so it was a dark space, with a rich assortment of smells. The toilets were situated in the open air, right in the bows of the ship (hence their nautical name, 'heads') with just six 'seats of ease' for about five hundred men!

Nelson, like most officers, slept in a specially constructed swinging box, or 'cot'. The original drapes (of which those shown are replicas) were made by his mistress, Lady Hamilton.

Disease

The *Victory* carried a surgeon who, with the help of his 'mates' (assistants) looked after the health of the crew. Disease was a constant problem and accounted for around half of the deaths in the British fleet (as opposed to a tenth caused by enemy action). But careful officers, like Nelson, took great care of the health of their men. For example, it was known that scurvy (a disease caused by vitamin C deficiency) could be kept in check by the use of onions and citrus fruits and, in 1804 alone 21,300 oranges and 81,685 onions were supplied to Nelson's Mediterranean fleet. As a result of this remarkable feat of logistics, his ships had by far the best sick record in the whole fleet.

Additionally, the sick were given special care in the sick bay which, in the *Victory*, was situated at the forward end of the upper gun-deck. Here, it was heated by the chimney-stack coming from the galley on the deck below and was also conveniently close to a special 'seat of ease' sheltered from the elements by a small structure known, because of its shape, as the 'roundhouse'.

Food

Each crew member on the *Victory* was entitled to a generous daily ration of food and drink. Two cold meals were served each day together with one main hot meal, prepared in the ship's 'galley' or kitchen. A typical daily menu would have been cold oatmeal porridge for breakfast, a salted meat stew for lunch and a supper of biscuits and cheese, washed down with half a pint of rum, mixed with water and issued in two parts (half at midday and half in the evening).

The officers ate rather better, because they were allowed to keep their own supplies and to have their meals cooked separately. Both the Captain and the Admiral held regular dinner parties to which their juniors were invited in rotation.

In order to keep a ship's company fed for weeks on end huge quantities of provisions were required. They were stored, mostly in wooden barrels, in the vast ship's hold beneath the waterline. Preservation methods were very primitive and so, wherever the ship went, her commanding officer and Purser were on the lookout for supplies of fresh food. Livestock, such as cattle, pigs and crates of hens and ducks, together with cows and goats for fresh milk, were kept in a special enclosure on the lower gun-deck known as the 'manger'.

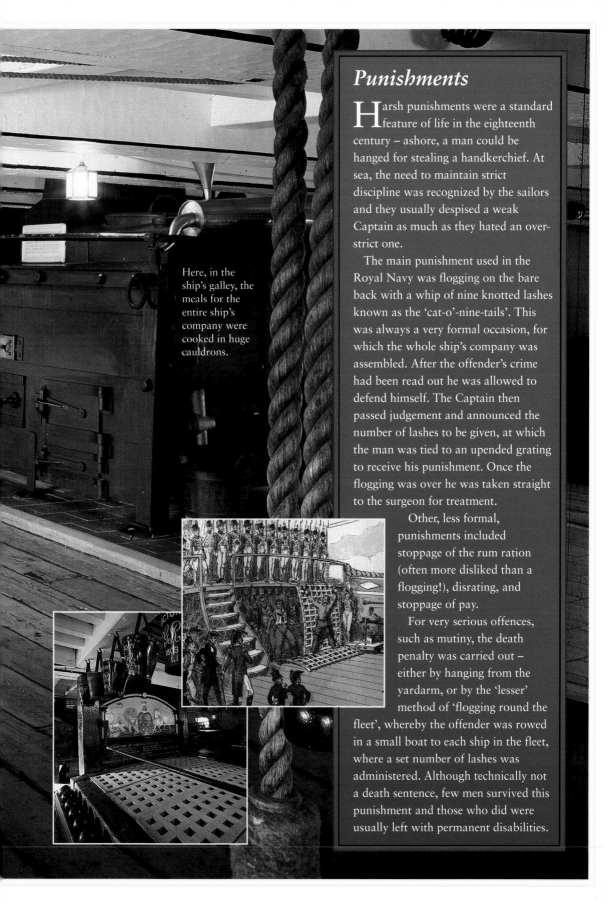

Here, in the ship's galley, the meals for the entire ship's company were cooked in huge cauldrons.

Punishments

Harsh punishments were a standard feature of life in the eighteenth century – ashore, a man could be hanged for stealing a handkerchief. At sea, the need to maintain strict discipline was recognized by the sailors and they usually despised a weak Captain as much as they hated an over-strict one.

The main punishment used in the Royal Navy was flogging on the bare back with a whip of nine knotted lashes known as the 'cat-o'-nine-tails'. This was always a very formal occasion, for which the whole ship's company was assembled. After the offender's crime had been read out he was allowed to defend himself. The Captain then passed judgement and announced the number of lashes to be given, at which the man was tied to an upended grating to receive his punishment. Once the flogging was over he was taken straight to the surgeon for treatment.

Other, less formal, punishments included stoppage of the rum ration (often more disliked than a flogging!), disrating, and stoppage of pay.

For very serious offences, such as mutiny, the death penalty was carried out – either by hanging from the yardarm, or by the 'lesser' method of 'flogging round the fleet', whereby the offender was rowed in a small boat to each ship in the fleet, where a set number of lashes was administered. Although technically not a death sentence, few men survived this punishment and those who did were usually left with permanent disabilities.

Rewards

The rates of pay were one of the most common causes of discontent among the sailors. In 1805 an Able Seaman received only £16 5s 6d (the equivalent in today's money of about £12,000) a year, whereas his colleague in the merchant service could earn almost half as much again.

The one major advantage of service in the Royal Navy was the possibility of earning prize money. When an enemy ship was captured, it was sold and the proceeds of the sale distributed among the officers and men of the ship which had made the capture. The officers received the lion's share but, even so, after a successful battle the Ordinary Seamen could expect to receive the equivalent of several months' pay. For example, after Trafalgar, the men of HMS *Victory* were each paid a total of £6 6s (about £4,000) in prize money.

If a man were injured while on active service, or wounded in battle, the details of his injury were entered on a 'hurt certificate', which entitled him to a pension. Alternatively, he could

Ordinary Seaman George Aunger (see 'The Ship Hierarchy') received these medals during his service career. The Naval General Service Medal (left) and Mr Boulton's medal (far right) were for Trafalgar. They are lying on a ledger recording the award of his Trafalgar prize money — £4 12s. 6d. (about £3,000 in today's money).

apply for a place in the special seamen's hospital at Greenwich.

Official campaign medals, as we know them today, did not exist at the beginning of the nineteenth century, although Admirals and Captains received special gold medals from the King for victory in major battles such as Trafalgar. There were, however, a number of unofficial awards. Lloyd's underwriters, for instance, set up a fund to pay for beautifully decorated swords to be presented to deserving officers. After the Battle of Trafalgar a Birmingham industrialist, Matthew Boulton, gave every officer and man who fought in the battle a private medal, produced at his own expense – Nelson's prize agent, Alexander Davison, gave a similar medal to each member of the *Victory*'s crew. An official campaign medal was not issued until 1847 – and then to survivors only, most of whom were fairly elderly by then.

THE BATTLE OF TRAFALGAR

Trafalgar was the final and decisive blow in a long campaign by Britain to thwart a major threat of invasion by France. In so doing, it also established Britain as the dominant world seapower and began a long process of erosion which led, eventually, to the collapse of the French Empire and the downfall of Napoleon in 1815.

The Campaign

In the early summer of 1805 Napoleon launched an ambitious plan to invade England, involving a concentration of all his available warships, a huge flotilla of transports and a specially raised army. But he never fully understood that fleets cannot be moved around at will like bodies of soldiers; as a result, he was decisively out-manoeuvred by the British naval commanders, who were thoroughly at home in sea warfare. Angrily, the French Emperor abandoned his transports in the French Channel ports, turned his army round and marched to subdue Austria.

The large fleet he had assembled was, however, still concentrated in the Spanish port of Cadiz. This powerful force, comprising thirty-three French and Spanish battleships, still posed a major threat and had to be eliminated. Vice Admiral Lord Nelson, who had been enjoying a brief spell of leave in England after playing a vital role in the campaign to beat off the invasion threat, was sent out in HMS *Victory* to take command of a fleet that had been specially gathered off Cadiz.

HMS *Victory*, anchored off the Isle of Wight, fires a salute as Vice Admiral Lord Nelson arrives in his barge on 14 September 1805 to begin the voyage south to take command of the British fleet off Cadiz.

A contemporary French print offers some fanciful ideas as to how England might be invaded, including balloons — and an early version of the Channel Tunnel! (Reproduced by courtesy of the Bibliothèque Nationale, Paris)

Planning the Battle

Nelson was then at the height of his powers. Widely recognized, even by Napoleon, as Britain's most successful commander, he was loved by the people at home as much as by the men who served under him. His arrival off Cadiz caused great excitement in the fleet and there was a sense that the decisive moment was approaching.

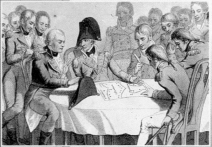

On 19 October the allied French and Spanish fleet sailed from Cadiz under the command of the French Vice Admiral Pierre de Villeneuve. The British fleet of twenty-seven battleships shadowed it until it was well clear of the port and then, on the morning of 21 October, off Cape Trafalgar, moved in to attack.

Nelson had spent the preceding days briefing his captains at dinner parties in the dining cabin of the *Victory*. Subsequently he issued a special memorandum setting out his tactics in detail. Knowing that he was outnumbered, he aimed to attack in three divisions. These would break through the allied line in three different places, dividing it into smaller and separate groups, each of which would then be forced to fight a separate battle. It was a high-risk plan, but Nelson relied on the superior morale of his crews and on the fact that they were better trained in gunnery, and so could maintain a far more deadly rate of fire than their opponents.

As the Battle of Trafalgar reaches its climax, at about 2.30 p.m., the *Victory* disengages from the French ship *Redoutable*, which has just surrendered after gallant resistance (painting by Harold Wyllie, after W.L. Wyllie).

The *Victory* mounted two massive 68-pounder carronnades in her bows. These heavy short-range guns, nicknamed 'smashers', were used to terrible effect in the close-quarter fighting at Trafalgar.

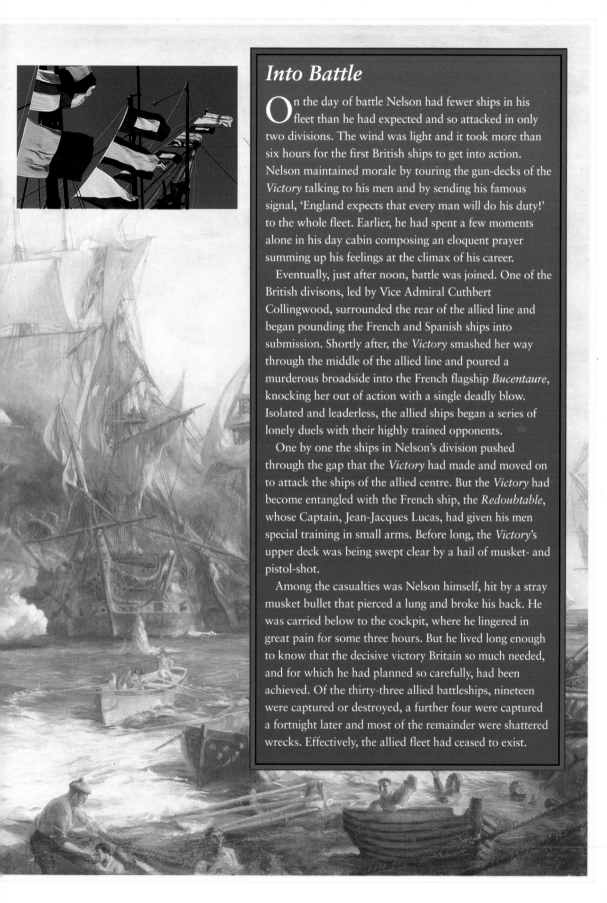

Into Battle

On the day of battle Nelson had fewer ships in his fleet than he had expected and so attacked in only two divisions. The wind was light and it took more than six hours for the first British ships to get into action. Nelson maintained morale by touring the gun-decks of the *Victory* talking to his men and by sending his famous signal, 'England expects that every man will do his duty!' to the whole fleet. Earlier, he had spent a few moments alone in his day cabin composing an eloquent prayer summing up his feelings at the climax of his career.

Eventually, just after noon, battle was joined. One of the British divisons, led by Vice Admiral Cuthbert Collingwood, surrounded the rear of the allied line and began pounding the French and Spanish ships into submission. Shortly after, the *Victory* smashed her way through the middle of the allied line and poured a murderous broadside into the French flagship *Bucentaure*, knocking her out of action with a single deadly blow. Isolated and leaderless, the allied ships began a series of lonely duels with their highly trained opponents.

One by one the ships in Nelson's division pushed through the gap that the *Victory* had made and moved on to attack the ships of the allied centre. But the *Victory* had become entangled with the French ship, the *Redoubtable*, whose Captain, Jean-Jacques Lucas, had given his men special training in small arms. Before long, the *Victory*'s upper deck was being swept clear by a hail of musket- and pistol-shot.

Among the casualties was Nelson himself, hit by a stray musket bullet that pierced a lung and broke his back. He was carried below to the cockpit, where he lingered in great pain for some three hours. But he lived long enough to know that the decisive victory Britain so much needed, and for which he had planned so carefully, had been achieved. Of the thirty-three allied battleships, nineteen were captured or destroyed, a further four were captured a fortnight later and most of the remainder were shattered wrecks. Effectively, the allied fleet had ceased to exist.

Nelson's Prayer

May the great God, whom I worship, grant to my Country, and for the benefit of Europe in general, a great and glorious Victory; and may no misconduct, in any one, tarnish it; and may humanity after victory be the predominant feature in the British Fleet.

For myself individually, I commit my life to Him who made me and may His blessing light upon my endeavours for serving my Country faithfully.

To Him I resign myself and the just cause which is entrusted to me to defend.

AMEN, AMEN, AMEN

The Battle of Trafalgar

12 Noon, 21 October 1805

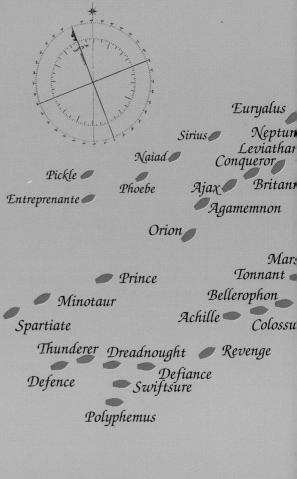

Africa

Euryalus

Sirius

Neptun

Naiad

Leviathan

Conqueror

Pickle

Phoebe

Ajax

Britann

Entreprenante

Agamemnon

Orion

Mars

Prince

Tonnant

Minotaur

Bellerophon

Achille

Spartiate

Colossu

Thunderer

Dreadnought

Revenge

Defence

Defiance

Swiftsure

Polyphemus

Wind Direction

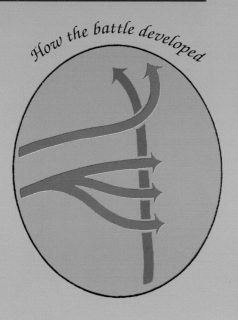

How the battle developed

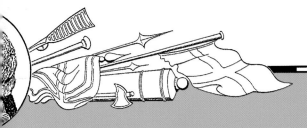

Neptuno

Scipion

Intrepide

Formidable

Mont-Blanc

Duguay-Trouin

Rayo

S. Francisco de Asis

S. Augustin

Héros

S. Trinidad

VICTORY

Bucentaure

Téméraire

Redoutable

S. Justo

Neptune

S. Leandro

Royal Sovereign

Indomptable

Belleisle

S. Ana

Fougueux

Monarca

Pluton

Algésiras

Bahama

Aigle

Montañes

Swiftsure

Argonaute

Argonauta

Ildefonso

Achille

P. de Asturias

Berwick

San Juan de Nepomuceno

Portsmouth

Bay of
Biscay

PORTUGAL

SPAIN

SPAIN

Cadiz

Gibraltar

CAPE
TRAFALGAR

Cape Spartel

Tetuan

AFRICA

Aftermath

The *Victory* had been exposed to the concentrated fire of five allied ships for over an hour during the long and risky approach into battle and she was very badly damaged. None the less, her crew insisted on their right to take home to England the body of their beloved commander, which had been specially preserved in a cask of spirits of brandy. So, after some temporary repairs at Gibraltar, the *Victory* limped slowly home, finally arriving at Spithead on 4 December. She then went up-Channel, to Sheerness, where the body was finally landed. After lying in state in the Painted Hall at Greenwich Hospital, it was carried up the River Thames in a spectacular water-borne procession and then to St Paul's Cathedral, where it was laid to rest in a tomb directly beneath the great dome.

The battered old ship returned to her birthplace, Chatham, where she underwent the second major refit of her long career. Her steering-wheel, shot away during the battle, was replaced with one bearing the words of Nelson's famous signal; while a special plaque was placed at the spot on the quarterdeck where he fell. So began the *Victory*'s long career as a shrine to the memory of Britain's greatest naval hero and of the men who fought with him at Trafalgar.

The Navy's shrine: the spot where Nelson died in the cockpit, below the waterline, is the scene of a special commemorative ceremony every Trafalgar Day.

A modern replica of the Victory's wheel, which was shot away during the battle. In front of the wheel is the 'binnacle' which houses the ship's compass.

With flags at half-mast, the *Victory* (centre) arrives back at Spithead, off Portsmouth, with the body of Nelson on board in December 1805 (painting by John Carmichael).

RESTORATION

The *Victory* was finally taken out of active service in 1812 and placed 'in ordinary' in Portsmouth Harbour. In 1823 she was again repaired and fitted out as the flagship of the Port Admiral. She was moored close to the harbour entrance and remained there throughout the rest of the nineteenth century.

In 1824 the custom began of holding a Trafalgar Anniversary Dinner on board and, on Trafalgar Day itself, the 'England Expects' signal was hoisted, together with a set of laurel wreaths. These customs are still continued today.

From time to time she was given repairs, including the fitting of lighter, metal masts, but time was taking its toll and, by 1921 she was very close to her end. The Society for Nautical Research decided to launch a national appeal for funds to save her and, in 1922, she was moved to her present resting place, Number 2 Dock, in the heart of the eighteenth-century section of Portsmouth Dockyard.

By now, successive refits had completely changed her appearance and the decision was taken to restore her to her condition at the Battle of Trafalgar. Eventually, after six years of careful research and restoration, she was opened to the public by King George V on 17 July 1928. She soon became a leading tourist attraction and a symbol of Britain's maritime heritage.

But she still needed much careful attention. Bomb damage during the Second World War, and the ravages of the death-watch beetle, all took their toll and by the mid 1970s she was in urgent need of another extensive refit. Rather than take her out of service, it was decided to carry out the work *in situ* by gradual stages.

That refit is still under way. As well as carrying out essential repairs, the opportunity is being taken to carry out more research into what her internal layout might have looked like and to restore her as close as possible to her 1805 condition.

It is hoped that she will be fully restored in time for the Trafalgar bicentenary celebrations in 2005.

The great marine artist, W.L. Wyllie, who was closely involved in the restoration of the *Victory* in the 1920s, captures the moment when the replica figurehead was unveiled.